Ripley's——o Believe It or Not!®

Developed and produced by Ripley Publishing Ltd

This edition published and distributed by:

Mason Crest
370 Reed Road, Broomall, Pennsylvania 19008
www.masoncrest.com

Printed and bound in the United States of America.

First printing
9 8 7 6 5 4 3 2 1

Ripley's Believe It or Not!
Fun Animals
ISBN-13: 978-1-4222-2569-1 (hardcover)
ISBN-13: 978-1-4222-9244-0 (e-book)
Ripley's Believe It or Not!—Complete 16 Title Series
ISBN-13: 978-1-4222-2560-8

Library of Congress Cataloging-in-Publication Data

Fun animals.
   p. cm. — (Ripley's believe it or not!)
ISBN 978-1-4222-2569-1 (hardcover) — ISBN 978-1-4222-2560-8 (series hardcover) — ISBN 978-1-4222-9244-0 (ebook)
 1. Animals—Miscellanea—Juvenile literature. 2. Curiosities and wonders—Juvenile literature. I. Title: Fun animals.
 QL49.S32 2013
 590—dc23
                    2012020341

PUBLISHER'S NOTE
While every effort has been made to verify the accuracy of the entries in this book, the Publisher's cannot be held responsible for any errors contained in the work. They would be glad to receive any information from readers.

WARNING
Some of the stunts and activities in this book are undertaken by experts and should not be attempted by anyone without adequate training and supervision.

Disbelief and Shock!

FUN ANIMALS

www.MasonCrest.com

FUN ANIMALS

Crazy critters. Meet some of the most

outrageous creatures in the world inside this book.

Open up to find the surfing rat, the family who keeps

a hippo in their house, and custom-made

luxury palaces for dogs!

Photographer Chris Van Wyk discovered
this funky punk-haired Mary River Turtle in
Australia in 2008.

Bioluminescence

Venture out at night and you might see some of the unbelievable organisms that look like regular citizens of the natural kingdom in the light, but can produce stunning luminous colors in the darkness.

Incendiary Insects

Both the male and female firefly have vivid luminous bodies that can easily be spotted in bushes at night. The female has only one bioluminescent glowing segment, and the male has larger eyes to help him to see it. He also has two bright body segments of his own, which flash in a regular pattern to attract a mate.

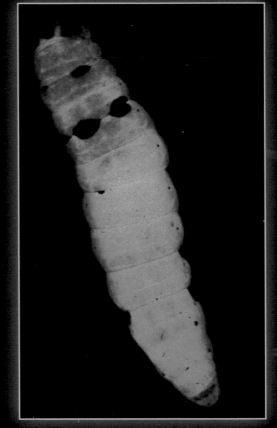

Death Light

Moth grubs don't glow until they're dying. The light is not from the grub itself but from bacteria expelled by a roundworm that burrows into it. The bacteria spread and digest the grub from the inside, turning it into a luminous corpse, before the worm swallows both and lays eggs in the dead larva.

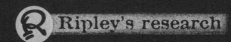

Ripley's research

Bioluminescence is the result of chemical reactions that convert energy into visible light. It has evolved in different creatures and organisms for various reasons, including communication, to warn predators off, to lure unsuspecting prey, and to attract mates. The natural light can also provide camouflage in the ocean, as some deep-sea creatures hide from predators below by blending in with the brighter water above.

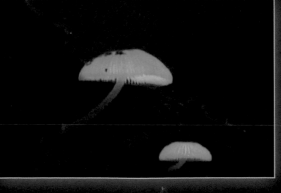

Fiery Fungi

Many types of mushrooms, including these Australian fungi, can glow brightly in the right conditions. Just don't pick one; they are usually as toxic as their color suggests.

Deep-sea Dazzler

The Tetrorchis is a type of jellyfish about ¾ in (1.9 cm) long. Bright bioluminescence in the creature, along with its thin tissue layers, produces a rainbow effect similar to oil on water.

A kitten was born in Perth, Australia, in November 2008 with two faces—giving it two mouths, four eyes, and two noses. The kitten was able to meow out of both mouths simultaneously.

TRAINED FISH ■ Researchers at the Marine Biological Laboratory at Wood's Hole, Massachusetts, have been training fish to catch themselves by using a recognizable tone to lure them into a net. The trained fish would be released into the ocean, and once they have reached market size they would be enticed into an underwater cage on hearing a tone they associate with food.

NORTH FACING ■ Scientists from the University of Duiburg-Essen, Germany, have deduced that cows automatically point north because they have their own built-in compasses—a relic from the days when their bovine ancestors needed a reliable sense of direction to migrate across the plains of Africa, Asia, and Europe.

DINOSAUR DUNG ■ A pile of dinosaur dung 130 million years old was sold at a New York auction for $960 in April 2008. The fossilized dung, from the Jurassic era, was bought by Steve Tsengas of Fairport Harbor, Ohio, to motivate employees in his company that treats dog and cat feces.

Micro Magic

Baby bird or extra terrestrial? With this picture of a chicken embryo—an entry in a competition to find the best miniature science photographs—it is hard to tell. It demonstrates the art of "Photomicrography" whereby scientists use microscopes and computers to capture stunning close-ups of life that is too small for the naked eye to see. The subjects are often dyed so their structures can be seen more clearly, hence the bright color of this bug-eyed bird.

INSECT INSPECTORS

Bees are being trained to sniff out bombs by U.S. scientists in New Mexico. The insects, which have a highly developed sense of smell, are rewarded with sugar water when they detect explosives. They are strapped into specially designed containers that leave their heads exposed so that they can be observed closely—when the bees smell the scent of explosives in the air they wave their proboscises around, expecting their reward.

VITAL VENOM ■ Researchers in California believe that scorpion venom can be used in the body to transport chemicals that attack brain tumors. Initial trials show that a peptide found in the venom of the giant yellow Israeli scorpion can be used to target aggressive tumors by delivering radioactive iodine that destroys the tumor tissue.

SHEEP SHADES ■ U.K.-based artist Julia Lohmann makes lampshades from sheep's stomachs. She buys the discarded stomachs from her local butcher for $10 and, following the insertion of a balloon to give it a bulbous shape, converts the organ into a lampshade, which she sells for $500.

BIG BIRD ■ A dinosaur recently discovered to have lived in Inner Mongolia, China, named *Gigantoraptor erlianensis*, stood up to 16 ft (4.8 m) tall, had a toothless beak, and may have been covered in feathers.

COMPUTER BEAVER ■ Artist Kasey McMahon from Los Angeles, California, has invented the Compubeaver—a computer housed in a dead beaver! She bought the beaver ready-stuffed and cut out the foam interior with an electric carving knife. After inserting the computer tower, she reinforced the animal with fiberglass.

JUMBO CALCULATOR ■ Studies carried out on elephants at a Tokyo zoo suggest that they are smarter than humans at mental math. In a test that involved dropping varying numbers of apples into two buckets and recording how often the participants correctly chose the bucket with the most fruit, the elephants scored 74 percent against the humans' 67 percent. In fact, one Indian elephant, Ashya, scored an amazing 87 percent.

SUPER SWIMMER ■ Saltwater crocodiles measure up to 23 ft (7 m) long and can swim at speeds of 18 mph (29 km/h) in short bursts—that's more than four times faster than a human swimming champion. Even on land they can run almost as fast as humans.

WHAT A BUZZ ■
The Africanized or "Killer" bee was accidentally released in Brazil in the 1950s and now swarms across South America and the southern United States. Killer bees are far more aggressive than the European honey bee and will even wait for you to surface if you hide underwater.

LETHAL LIONS ■
In 1898, two man-eating lions ate 28 railway workers and a number of local people in Kenya.

BIG BITE ■
An adult hippopotamus can open its mouth so wide that a 4-ft-tall (1.2-m) child could stand inside. It possesses such powerful jaws that it could bite a 12-ft-long (3.6-m) crocodile in half.

SLEEPY STING ■
Even when dead, a jellyfish can sting, and the sting from the Australian box jellyfish can kill a human in just four minutes.

SHARKS OF STEEL ■
Sharks can detect one part of blood in 100 million parts of water; the biggest —such as the Great White—can bite through steel cables.

Wild Ride!

It may look like he is hunting for his next meal, but this lion has been trained to ride on the back of a horse in an amazing display for visitors at a zoo in Xiamen, China. Tigers also hitch a ride on horses as part of the show. The horse is protected from the big cat's claws by a rug on its back.

MINI EGG ■ Andy Jarrell of Taylorsville, North Carolina, discovered a fully developed chicken egg smaller than a grape in his chicken coop in December 2007.

HORSEPITAL VISITOR ■ In a bid to cheer up a sick relative in Hawaii's Wilcox Memorial Hospital in 2008, a man tried to take the patient's favorite horse into the ward. Horse and man were eventually stopped by security guards on the third floor.

ARROW ORDEAL ■ Lucky Jack, a dog from Hot Springs Village, Arkansas, was shot through the head with an arrow and survived—without any permanent damage. He lived with the steel-tipped arrowhead in his jaw for five months until it could be surgically removed.

BLOODSUCKERS ■ Female fleas can drink 15 times their weight in blood every day. Fleas can also pull 160,000 times their own bodyweight, the equivalent of a human pulling 2,679 double-decker buses.

NO LUNGS ■ A species of frog discovered in a remote corner of Indonesia in 2007 has no lungs and breathes through its skin. Scientists believe the aquatic frog *Barbourula kalimantanensis* has adapted itself to reduce its buoyancy in order to keep from being swept down the fast-moving rivers where it lives.

SIX-LEGGED ■ A six-legged deer with two tails was found in the wild near Armuchee, Georgia, in 2008. Animal experts believe it had an identical twin that didn't form completely.

UNICORN BORN ■ In 2008, a nature reserve in Tuscany, Italy, claimed the world's first unicorn deer after a roe deer was born with a single horn in the center of its head. The condition that conjured up images of the mythological creature is thought to have been caused by a genetic flaw in the deer. Its twin was born with the usual two horns.

DRACULA BIRD ■ The ground finch of the Galapagos Islands is a vampire. Using its sharp beak, it pecks holes in the wings of nesting masked boobies and drinks their blood.

SPLIT LEG ■ Angel, a dog from Cleveland, Ohio, was born with a split leg. Her lower leg parts are located side by side, rather than end to end, giving the impression that she has five legs.

Snappy Surgeon

Beatrice Langevin performed the world's first major surgery on the jaw of a crocodile after it was badly injured in a fierce fight on a crocodile farm in Pierrelatte, France. The veterinary surgeon put a plank of wood in the jaws of the 12-ft (3.7-m) creature and used a regular domestic drill to perform the operation.

SERPENT VILLAGE ■ A village in India boasts one snake to every two people. The 6,000 villagers of Choto Pashla, West Bengal, share their habitat with as many as 3,000 snakes—mainly highly venomous monocled cobras, which can grow up to 6 ft (1.8 m) long. Not surprisingly, neighboring villagers are scared to visit.

PIGEON FANCIER ■ A monkey in China found salvation by developing a close friendship with a pigeon. Abandoned by his mother, the baby macaque was close to death when taken to an animal hospital in Goangdong Province in 2007 but pulled through after bonding with his new feathered friend. The two became inseparable.

RADIO FROG ■ Researchers at the University of Illinois have discovered that the concave-eared torrent frog, from China, can tune its ears to different sound frequencies—like tuning in to a radio. Its selective hearing, achieved by opening and closing eardrum canals, enables it to listen to high-frequency mating sounds against the low-frequency noise of rushing water in its habitat.

HERBAL REMEDY ■ Orangutans in Indonesia have been observed preparing their own plant-based soothing balm. They have been seen to pick a handful of leaves from a plant, chew the leaves, and use saliva to produce a soapy foam. Then they scoop some of the lather in their hand and apply it to their arm, as if putting on sunscreen. The leaf is not part of the orangutans' usual diet, but local people are aware of its anti-inflammatory properties.

HIPPO
in the House

FUN ANIMALS

Ripley's — Believe It or Not!®

DID YOU KNOW?

> While young hippos are buoyant and swim quite happily, heavy adult hippos can't actually swim at all. They can hold their breath for up to six minutes at a time and move through the water by pushing off the bottom. They can sleep underwater and surface for air automatically without waking up.

> Despite their huge bulk and the time they spend in the water, hippos can easily outrun a human on land. They can reach speeds of up to 30 mph (50 km/h).

> The oldest living hippo in captivity is 57-year-old Donna, who resides in a zoo in Evansville, Indiana. She has a while to go to clinch the record for the oldest ever, held by a hippo that lived to the age of 61 in a zoo in Germany.

> After the elephant and the white rhino, the hippo is the third largest land animal, with some adult males reaching 8,000 lb (3,628 kg) in weight.

Imagine sharing your home with a one-ton teenage hippo, complete with huge appetite, who eats up to 175 lb (80 kg) of food a day.

That was the task facing the South African couple who took on an unusual addition to their family almost ten years ago. Park ranger Tonie Joubert and his wife Shirley discovered Jessica the hippo on the banks of a river in Limpopo Province when she was only a few hours old. She weighed a mere 35 lb (16 kg) and still had her umbilical cord attached.

She had been swept away from her mother in devastating floods that hit Mozambique and South Africa in 2000. Knowing that young hippos stay with their mothers for at least four years in the wild, the Jouberts decided to take Jessica home.

They gave the young hippo heavy-duty massages and allowed her to wander about the house before she grew prohibitively large, breaking beds in the house three times.

Over time, Jessica moved out to join the wild hippos that visit the Joubert residence, but she still lives close by her adopted family and when they return from a trip they often find her waiting by the house for a meal. Jessica still eats some of her meals in the house—she's allowed in the kitchen and the lounge—and drinks more than 2½ gal (10 l) of coffee a day.

CHICKEN SWEATERS ■ Jo Eglen, from Norwich, Norfolk, England, has rescued 1,500 chickens from factory farms—and has had woolly sweaters knitted for each of them to protect them from the cold. Many factory farm birds lose their plumage because of stress.

WOLF POSTER ■ Unable to afford another dog after his old one died, shepherd Du Hebing from Xi'an City, China, controls his flock of sheep using just a poster of a wolf.

CONTACT LENSES ■ The eyesight of a 15-year-old cat from the Isle of Wight, England, has been restored by fitting the animal with contact lenses. Ernest suffered from a condition whereby his lids turned inward and scratched his eyeballs, and veterinarians suggested the innovative solution because he was too old to risk an operation.

BAT LATTE ■ A woman from Iowa drank a pot of coffee, unaware that a dead bat was inside the filter. After drinking the coffee in the morning, she discovered the bat only that night when she went to clean the filter.

GREEN BLOOD ■ A new species of frog with green blood and turquoise bones has been discovered in Cambodia. The Samkos bush frog owes its unusual coloring to biliverdin, a pigment that is usually processed in the liver as a waste product but, in the case of this frog, is passed back into the bloodstream. The green blood helps with the frog's camouflage and makes it taste unpleasant to predators.

SCOOBY IN COURT ■ A dog named Scooby appeared as a courtroom witness during criminal proceedings in 2008. The animal is thought to have been with his owner when she was found dead in her Paris, France, apartment, and on being led into the witness box he barked furiously at a suspect who was led into the room.

MIGHTY MOUSE ■ A little mouse that was put into a viper's cage as a tasty snack for the venomous snake turned the tables and killed the snake instead. The mouse repeatedly attacked the 14-in (35-cm) viper in the cage in Nantou, Taiwan, and after a 30-minute fight, incredibly, the snake was dead and the brave little mouse was left with hardly a scratch.

MONKEY MINDER ■ An orphaned monkey that was being bullied by bigger monkeys was given its own guard dog at Jiaozuo City Zoo in China. Whenever it felt threatened, the baby monkey would jump on the dog's back and hold tight until the bullies gave up.

MONKEY WAITERS ■ A sake restaurant near Tokyo, Japan, employs two monkeys as waiters. One of the macaques takes customers' drinks orders and brings them to their table while the other hands the customers hot towels. The animals receive tips of boiled soya beans.

SNAKE MASSAGE ■ For $80 a visit, customers at a spa in northern Israel can receive a snake massage. Ada Barak uses nonvenomous king and corn snakes to produce a relaxing kneading sensation over the face and body.

CHIPMUNK HOARD ■ When Hope Wideup of Demotte, Indiana, looked under the hood of her car to see why the indicator and windscreen wipers were not working and why the engine was making a strange noise, she found thousands of nuts that had been stored there by a chipmunk.

Hotel Trunks

They may look like unwanted guests, but staff at a hotel in Zambia have spent ten years since the lodge was built watching a herd of elephants wandering through the lobby. The hotel was built on the elephants' traditional route to a mango-tree feeding ground in South Luangwa National Park. For the four weeks when the mangos are ripe and ready for eating, the elephants make their way twice a day through the lodge. Guests are allowed to watch but are kept at a safe distance.

LUCKY BREAK ■ An Australian cat used up one of its nine lives in 2008 when it survived a 34-story fall from the window of a Queensland apartment building. Seven-year-old Voodoo liked to perch on a narrow ledge outside owner Sheree Washington's high-rise flat, but this time he toppled over the edge, and was saved only because he landed in some bushes.

FISH OUT OF WATER ■ After leaping from its bowl, a pet goldfish in Gloucester, England, somehow survived for 13 hours out of water. When Barbara Woodford found Ginger lying on the floor, she feared the worst, but once she put him back in water, he swam around happily. A goldfish expert said: "This is the longest I've heard of a goldfish staying alive out of water. It's quite astonishing."

SKIING APE ■ An orangutan at the Institute of Greatly Endangered and Rare Species in Miami keeps active by riding an inflatable jet ski. Four-year-old Surya wears a child's lifejacket to stay warm and to prevent him going underwater, because he doesn't like getting his head wet.

NO SALT ■ Although they often live their entire lives in saltwater, sea snakes cannot drink saltwater.

EXPERT MIMIC ■ A wild blackbird living in Weston-super-Mare, Somerset, England, is an expert mimic—and can copy the sounds of a cell phone, a car alarm, a wolf-whistle and even an ambulance siren.

POINTLESS TEETH ■ The whale shark, the world's largest fish, grows to be more than 60 ft (18 m) long and has thousands of teeth—but it doesn't bite anything.

Lizard Mystery

Peter Beaumont, a doctor from Darwin, Australia, cracked open an egg for dinner and found a dead lizard inside. He believes the tiny gecko may have crawled into the chicken to eat an embryo and become stuck. The egg then formed around the lizard.

PREDICTIVE TEXT ■ Elephants in Kenya send text messages as a warning if they are straying too near farms. The elephants have had cell phone SIM cards inserted into their collars and these automatically send text messages to rangers if they step out of the 90-acre (36-ha) Ol Pejeta conservancy.

FISHING PIG ■ A pig in China has learned how to catch fish from a pond. The pig steps into the shallow water of the specialist tropical fish pond in Zhenping, catches the fish in its mouth and eats them on the spot.

BUTT ID ■ Chimpanzees are able to identify other chimps by their butts. Research indicates that they probably identify animals they know by their entire bodies instead of just their faces—something that no other primates, including humans, are known to do.

WOMAN'S BEST FRIEND ■ Angelina the Labrador saved the life of her owner Maria Tripodi by knocking her out of the way just as the roof of her Rivoli, Italy, house collapsed. The dog probably felt tiny tremors too small for humans to detect.

SEX CHANGE ■ The Kushiro Municipal Zoo in Hokkaido, Japan, bought a male polar bear pup in 2005, only to find out three years later that it was a female.

NOSEY DOG ■ A poodle in Forli, Italy, bit off its owner's nose before running around the garden with it. Police chased the dog around Loredana Romano's garden before finally managing to retrieve the remains of the nose. Surgeons later reattached the chewed nose to Mrs. Romano who says she has forgiven her pet.

COUNTING BEES ■ By conducting controlled tests with nectar, researchers at the University of Queensland, Australia, have discovered that honey bees can count to four.

Swift Shrimp

An energetic crustacean was given a workout by scientists at a laboratory in Charleston, South Carolina, as part of an experiment. They discovered that the shrimp could run on an underwater treadmill nonstop for three hours.

www.ripleybooks.com
<<< go to >>>

GREEDY FISH

The Great Swallower fish certainly lives up to its name. A man fishing in the Cayman Islands spotted a dead 35-in-long (90-cm) Snake Mackerel that burst the expandable stomach of a Great Swallower measuring only 7 in (18 cm) in length. It's unknown how the smaller fish managed to swallow the predator without itself being eaten.

GREEDY SNAKE ■ A python bit off more than it could chew after attempting to swallow a fully grown wallaby on a university campus in Cairns, Australia, in November 2008. The beast had to give up on its meal and slithered off.

RATS' URINE ■ British children's author Emily Gravett made her work *The Little Mouse's Big Book of Fears* look more authentic by yellowing the pages with rats' urine. Gravett, who used to own two pet rats, also got them to chew the pages of the book to make it appear as if they had been nibbled by a nervous mouse.

FACING EXTINCTION ■ Polar bears could be extinct within 100 years owing to global warming. Arctic sea ice is melting at a rate of up to nine percent per decade, and Arctic summers could be ice-free by 2050. As the ice disappears, so will the polar bears' natural habitat.

COW TOWER ■ Designed by local artist Josée Perreault and perched high on a hill at St.-Georges-de-Windsor, Quebec, Canada, is an observation tower built in the shape of a cow lying in a field.

BLUE DUCKLINGS ■ In Kentucky, it is illegal to dye a duckling blue and offer it for sale unless more than six are for sale at once.

Deer in the City

You might not expect to see a reindeer accompanying a man on his daily business around a London suburb, but that's exactly what Dobbey does with owner Gordon Elliott, who takes his pet for walks in Enfield and rides on local trains each weekend of the winter holiday season.

GREEN BEARS ■ Three polar bears at a Japanese zoo turned temporarily green in 2008 after swimming in an algae-filled pond. The algae, which entered hollow spaces in the bears' normally white fur, infested the animals' enclosure following two months of particularly high temperatures.

RAM RAIDER ■ A 300-lb (130-kg) ram that lives with a family in Cardiff, Wales, has his own specially built bungalow, complete with carpet and windows. Rescued by David Palmer as a lamb in 2005, Nick the sheep is now so much a part of the family that he rides in the back seat of David's car and most evenings settles down on the sofa with him to watch television. He has also been known to raid the cookie jar by butting it until the contents spill out.

RODENT INTERLOPER ■ In 2008, a pet cat in Yantai City, China, adopted a rat and brought it up alongside her four kittens. The rat drank the cat's milk and also played happily with its new feline siblings.

BOOMERANG'S BACK ■ A pigeon that had been away for ten years returned home to the man who had raised her—and on Father's Day. Boomerang earned her name in 1998 when she flew the 1,200 mi (1,930 km) back to Dino Reardon's house in North Yorkshire, England, after being given to a breeder in Spain. Later that year, Mr. Reardon gave her to a friend in Lancashire, but she reappeared in June 2008. She inherited her homing instincts from her father, who once walked 60 mi (95 km) back home after having his wings clipped by thieves.

SINGING WOLVES ■ A Chinese zoo has formed a new singing group—made up of 30 wolves. Luo Yong, a keeper at Chongqing Wild Zoo, was amazed to discover the animals' musical ability when he was playing guitar and a young wolf began howling along to the rhythm and patting the strings with its claws. Next Luo Yong wants to teach them to dance, too!

DOG TIRED ■ Charlie, a standard poodle from Chilliwack, British Columbia, Canada, delivered a litter of no fewer than 16 puppies in March 2008. The exhausted dog gave birth to ten female and six male pups.

CLEVER CHIMP ■ Panzee, a highly intelligent chimpanzee from Georgia's Language Research Center, has a vocabulary of at least 150 English words. She is also able to use a computer to identify objects and even barters for food using symbols.

FLYING LESSONS ■ Gary Zammit of Cornwall, England, taught a bird to fly by running alongside it with food in his pockets, flapping his arms, squawking and pretending to try to take off. He found the orphaned baby gray heron after a storm, which killed the rest of its family. The heron, named Dude, eventually responded to his surrogate father's unusual tuition by copying his actions and then taking to the skies, first at a height of 3 ft (1 m) before graduating to 70 ft (21 m).

IT'S A HEXAPUS! ■ Henry, an octopus at an aquarium in Blackpool, England, was born with just six legs.

MUSICAL CAT ■ A cat in Philadelphia, Pennsylvania, has been playing the piano for more than three years. Adopted from an animal shelter, Nora, a gray tabby, moved into the home of music teacher Betsy Alexander and used to sit under the piano and watch intently until each lesson was over. Then one day she climbed up on the bench herself and began playing the keys with her paws. Playing piano became a daily routine and Nora's exploits were posted on the Internet, where they soon achieved more than ten million viewings. The musical cat also has her own CD, DVD, downloadable ringtone and line of e-cards.

THREE BEARS ■ A 350-lb (160-kg) brown bear and her two cubs walked into a crowded restaurant in Sinaia, Romania, in June 2008 and sat down at tables. As terrified diners abandoned their meals and fled, the three bears tucked into the leftovers before raiding the kitchen for more food.

Hen Hypnosis

Psychological counselor Xu Yiqiang demonstrated the art of hypnotizing chickens at a medical university in Xi'an, northwest China, in 2007. The bird lay motionless after a series of gestures and massages until released from its trance.

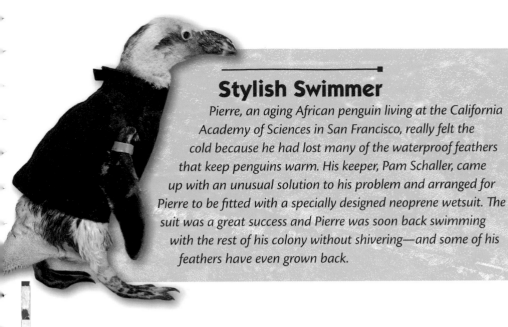

Stylish Swimmer

Pierre, an aging African penguin living at the California Academy of Sciences in San Francisco, really felt the cold because he had lost many of the waterproof feathers that keep penguins warm. His keeper, Pam Schaller, came up with an unusual solution to his problem and arranged for Pierre to be fitted with a specially designed neoprene wetsuit. The suit was a great success and Pierre was soon back swimming with the rest of his colony without shivering—and some of his feathers have even grown back.

ARTIFICIAL BEAK ■ A bald eagle was given an artificial beak by Idaho veterinarians in 2008 after its real one was shot off by a hunter. The bird, named Beauty, was found scrounging for food and slowly starving at a landfill site in Alaska in 2005. Without a beak, it had been impossible for her to pick up food, drink or preen her feathers.

HOMICIDAL HORNETS ■ The Japanese giant hornet can kill 40 honey bees in just one minute, thanks to its large mandibles, which can swiftly decapitate a bee. It takes only half a dozen of these hornets a little more than two hours to exterminate the entire population of a 30,000-member hive.

Deer Dane

Cindy the baby roe deer found an unlikely father figure in Rocky the Great Dane when she was found wet, cold, and close to death by staff at the Secret World Rescue Centre in Somerset, England. The fawn was cared for before leaving her 125-lb (57-kg) companion to join a deer herd in the wild.

www.ripleybooks.com >>>> go to

Twisted Tails

One of the best examples of a mysterious "Rat King" is on display at the Otago Museum in Dunedin, New Zealand. It was found in the 1930s in a shipping shed. The strange specimens are formed when the tails of several rats become tied together in a knot in the nest and they cannot free themselves. Despite expert research, nobody is sure how this happens or if it is even a natural occurrence.

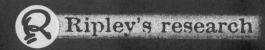
RAT KINGS

Rat Kings are an unexplained phenomena with the earliest report dating back to the 16th century. Some experts think that rats become entangled when they are forced into a small space, with the animals naturally facing outward to protect themselves. Eventually, their tails become stuck together and they starve. Some believe that the specimens in museums are hoaxes, but people who have studied them say that the rats have broken tails and calluses that suggest that they were alive for a long period tangled together. The museum Mauritianum in Altenburg, Germany, owns the largest known mummified Rat King, which was found in 1828 and consists of 32 rats.

TRAPPED PIG ■ A pig survived for 36 days buried beneath rubble in the earthquake that devastated southwest China in May 2008. The pig, which lost two-thirds of its weight during its ordeal, existed on water and a bag of charcoal that had been buried alongside it in the ruins of Pengzhou City, Sichuan Province. Although charcoal has no nutritional value, it filled the pig up.

CHEWED TOE ■ A miniature dachshund chewed off its owner's right big toe in 2008 while she was asleep. Linda Floyd of Alton, Illinois, woke from a nap to find her toe missing. She had no feeling in her toes because of nerve damage from diabetes.

BACK BIRTH ■ Female Surinam toads of South America absorb their eggs into the skin of their backs, where the young remain until bursting forth as fully developed amphibians.

PAINFUL JOB ■ U.S. entomologist Justin Schmidt, who helped create the Schmidt Sting Pain Index, has been stung by about 150 different species of bugs on six different continents in the course of his research.

RAT TRAP ■ Pest control officers trapped and removed 788 rats from an infested house in Sutherlin, Oregon, in the spring of 2008.

PIGCASSO ■ Holding the brush in his mouth, Smithfield the pot-bellied pig has created hundreds of paintings, which sell for $16 each over the Internet. His proud owner, Fran Martin from Richmond, Virginia, says blue is his favorite color to paint with.

TEN-YEAR FAST ■ The olm, a cave-dwelling European amphibian, can live more than 58 years and survive a decade without food.

RAT REWARD ■ To mark the Year of the Rat in 2008, authorities in Kuala Lumpur, Malaysia, offered a bounty on rats, dead or alive.

CANINE TOOTH ■ An 11-year-old Brazilian boy bit a Pit Bull that attacked him—and lost a canine tooth in the process. Gabriel Almeida's tooth was dislodged when he grabbed the dog's neck and bit into it after the animal savaged him while he played in his uncle's backyard in Belo Horizonte in July 2008. Gabriel said later, "It is better to lose a tooth than one's life."

SURF'S UP

When 14-year-old Boomer Hodel of Haleiwa, Hawaii, took his pet rats to the beach to wash them, he never expected they would enjoy the experience so much that it would lead to a whole new hobby. The rats—Fin and Tofu—loved splashing around in the shallow water, so Boomer taught them how to surf and they now make regular trips to the beach with their custom-built surfboards to ride 4-ft (1.2-m) waves.

MONKEY PIG ■ A piglet born in China in 2008 had the face of a monkey! One of five piglets born to a sow owned by Feng Changlin of Xiping, the newborn had two thin lips, a small nose, two big eyes and its rear legs were considerably longer than its front ones, causing it to jump rather than walk. While Feng's family were too scared to look at it, villagers flocked from miles around to see the curiosity.

LONG HOP ■ Southern cricket frogs, which come from the southern U.S.A., can jump 36 times their own body length.

STRANGE FAMILY ■ The elephant shrews, or sengi, are a family of tiny, insect-eating African mammals that are more closely related to elephants than to shrews.

LIFESAVER ■ A dog saved his master's life in 2008 by fetching his cell phone. Albert Hoffman suffered serious back injuries and a punctured lung after falling 20 ft (6 m) from a tree while bird hunting in Upper Austria. Unable to move, he called for his pet Labrador to fetch his phone from his nearby backpack so that he could call emergency services.

BACK LEGS ■ A farmer from Kunming, China, was offered nearly $6,000 for a bull with six legs. Li Guolin says the 18-month-old bull, which was born with two small extra legs on its back, has become a tourist attraction.

CAMEL COMFORT ■ A tiny 18-oz (510-g) baby gibbon found starving to death after her mother failed to produce milk for her was nursed back to health with the help of a stuffed toy camel. The tiny, ten-day-old Sumatran Siamang gibbon was taken away from her mother at a zoo in Bristol, England, and given the soft toy camel to cuddle up to while being fed baby food.

MISS PIGGY ■ Nellie, a pig owned by pig trainers Steve and Priscilla Valentine of Gig Harbor, Washington State, can perform over 70 tricks. She can play baseball, golf, soccer and piano; she skateboards; she can put coins in a bank; and she can spell words. She is such a star that she even has her own credit cards. Priscilla Valentine started teaching her pet pigs tricks to keep them from getting bored. She says: "These animals are sensitive and Intelligent. They use logic. They're creative, in bad ways of course. They'll learn to open the refrigerator. Having a pig is like having a two-year-old child for 15 years."

Turtle Power

Amateur photographer Chris Van Wyk had quite a surprise when he spotted this punk turtle swimming in the Mary River in Queensland, Australia, in 2008. The unusual creature is an endangered Mary River Turtle and its crazy green "hair" is in fact algae growing on the turtle's head.

GARDEN DOLPHIN ■ In July 2008, a dead dolphin was found in the back garden of a house, perched high up a steep hill, half a mile (0.8 km) from the sea. Gary Harvey of Portland, Dorset, England, who saw the body of the 3-ft-long (1-m) dolphin lying there, said there was no tidal wave at the time.

FISHING CAT ■ The fishing cat, or *Felis viverrina*, of India, has water-resistant fur, webbed feet and dives headfirst into the water to catch fish.

EEL LIGHTS ■ The Aqua Toto Aquarium in Gifu, Japan, used an electric eel to power the lights on a Christmas tree in December 2007.

BEACHED WHALE ■ An 18-ft (5.5-m) minke whale, weighing around 12 tons, swam nearly 1,000 mi (1,600 km) up the Amazon River in November 2007, before beaching itself on a sandbar.

FEMALE PRESERVE ■ The Amazon molly, *Poecilia formosa*, of Texas and Mexico, is practically an all-female species of fish with no need of males for reproduction. Instead, it mates with males from a different species, but the offspring are clones of their mother and do not inherit any of the male's DNA.

FISH CATCH ■ Orangutans on the island of Kaja, Borneo, have developed the art of stabbing at fish using spears that the local fishermen have discarded.

TREE FISH ■ In times of drought, mangrove killifish, native to Florida and Central America, crawl up into trees and hide among the moist, rotting wood of branches and trunks. They temporarily change their biological makeup so they can breathe air, enabling them to survive out of water for several months of the year.

CATFISH SHUFFLE ■ A school of 30 catfish walked along a street in Pinellas County, Florida, in July 2008 after crawling out of a sewer that had become flooded by heavy rainfall. The catfish, which can travel on land provided they stay moist, propelled themselves along the street using their pectoral fins.

MONSTER SQUID ■ In 2008, New Zealand fishermen caught a colossal squid—*Mesonychoteuthis hamiltoni*—that was 33 ft (10 m) long and weighed 990 lb (450 kg). The monster specimen took two hours to land in Antarctic waters. One expert said that calamari rings made from it would be like tractor tires.

FALSE EYE ■ A miniature horse in Lawton, Oklahoma, that lost one of its eyes a few days after birth was fitted with a $3,000 prosthetic eye. The plastic eye was made from a mold of the horse's eye socket and was hand-painted to look exactly like the other eye, with deep blue features and tiny red veins.

DRUM BEAT ■ Low-frequency mating calls of the black drum fish of the eastern U.S.A. are so strong and loud that they can be heard in homes near the shore.

DOLPHIN GUIDE ■ In March 2008, a dolphin managed to rescue a pair of beached pygmy sperm whales at Mahia Beach, New Zealand, by remarkably leading them around a sand bar and then back out to sea.

HUGE HALIBUT ■ Fishing off Norway in 2008, Danish vacationer Soren Beck caught a giant Atlantic halibut. The monster fish weighed a massive 443 lb (200 kg) and was 8 ft 1 in (2.5 m) long— more than twice the size of an average halibut.

This small army of colorful lumpfish makes for an eye-catching display in the Tokyo aquarium where they swim.

TOY STORY ■ Louis, a giant Pacific octopus at the Blue Reef Aquarium in Newquay, Cornwall, England, becomes aggressive if someone comes too close to his favorite toy— a Mr. Potato Head.

PERPETUAL MOTION ■ Tuna fish never stop moving, swimming at a steady rate of 9 mph (14 km/h) for their entire life. Scientists estimate that a 15-year-old tuna will have swum more than one million miles (1.6 million km).

BALLOON SUCKERS

Lumpsuckers, or lumpfish, will take any opportunity to stick themselves to virtually anything, as they did when balloons were introduced into their tank at an aquarium in Tokyo, Japan. The fish get their name because of the pelvic fins under their body that they use as a "sucker" pad to attach themselves to rocks and seaweed. Such is the strength of their suction that scientists in the 18th century claimed that they could lift a bucket of water by a lumpfish attached to it!

Ripley's Believe It or Not!®
FUN ANIMALS
www.ripleys.com

Cage of Death

Have you ever wondered what it would be like to be stalked by a crocodile in its element? Visitors to Crocosaurus Cove in Darwin, Australia, have the chance to find out. Locked inside an acrylic tank a mere 1½ in (4 cm) thick and lowered into the water, they are companions of Choppa, an 18-ft (5.5-m) saltwater crocodile who lost his front feet fighting other crocodiles, but retains his formidable jaws to snap at the tantalizing snacks appearing in his pool.

DOG DRIVER ■ Charles McCowan left his truck in the parking lot of a convenience store in Azusa, California, in February 2008 with his 80-lb (36-kg) Boxer dog named Max in the front seat. When he emerged from the store a few minutes later to discover both truck and dog gone, he immediately reported the theft to the police. Shortly after the police arrived, they found the truck parked just across the street in front of a fast-food outlet with Max still in place. A security video showed that Max had accidentally knocked the gear shift into neutral, sending the truck sloping gently backward.

TRAMPOLINE ESCAPE ■ A dog escaped from his owner's garden in York, England, in June 2008 by bouncing over the fence on a child's trampoline. Harvey, a three-year-old Staffordshire bull terrier, bounced into a neighbor's garden but was free for only four days before he was found and returned home.

HOMING INSTINCT ■ Australian scientists have found that crocodiles have a built-in satellite navigation system to enable them to find their way home. Three crocodiles were monitored after being moved 250 mi (400 km) from their territory but, swimming between 6 and 19 mi (10 and 30 km) a day, they returned home within weeks.

TOAD'S ESCAPE ■ A cane toad emerged unharmed after being swallowed by a dog and spending 40 minutes in the animal's stomach. The toad was gobbled up in Darwin, Australia, in June 2008 by a dog that mistook it for a meat pie. The toad regained its freedom when the dog vomited it back up. The dog, too, had a lucky escape as cane toads have toxic glands in their skin which can kill animals that try to eat them. Fortunately, the dog swallowed the toad whole instead of chewing it.

FAT STORE ■ Crocodiles store fat in their tails, so they can go quite a while without eating—as long as two years in the case of some large adults.

GROUP ACTIVITY ■ White pelicans use teamwork to capture food. They surround fish and herd them into shallow water where they can feed on them more easily.

CROC'S BEER ■ When a crocodile wandered into a bar in Noonamah, Australia, in 2008, the regulars didn't run for cover—instead they gave it a beer. Then they taped up its mouth and put the 2-ft-long (60-cm) reptile in a box.

HELPFUL HOUND ■ A dachshund in Zhengzhou, China, has learned to push a wheelchair. Little Guai Guai takes his owner's father for a ride by running underneath the wheelchair with his hind legs on the ground and his front legs pushing the foot rests. He is so small and fast that most passersby assume the wheelchair is motorized.

SIR PENGUIN ■ A penguin at Edinburgh Zoo, Scotland, received a knighthood from the Norwegian Army in 2008. Nils Olav, a King penguin, is the mascot of the Norwegian King's Guard and inspects the troops when they perform at Edinburgh's Military Tattoo.

SCUBA-DIVING CAT ■ Whereas most cats steer clear of water, Hawkeye has gone scuba-diving with her owner on more than 20 expeditions. Gene Alba has built a special diving suit so that Hawkeye can join him beneath the surface of his swimming pool in Redding, California. An air tube connects his own oxygen tank with the cat's glass mask, enabling her to stay underwater for up to an hour. Alba reckons that, provided her face is dry, Hawkeye is happy in her new pastime—particularly if it means putting one over on Mutley, his scuba-diving dog.

SIXTH SENSE ■ Sharks and rays have an extra sense, courtesy of the ampullae of Lorenzini, special organs that enable them to detect electromagnetic fields. Whenever a living creature moves, it generates an electrical field and Great White sharks are so sensitive they can detect half a billionth of a volt in the water.

TURTLE POWER ■ A leatherback turtle swam 12,774 mi (20,560 km) in 647 days from Indonesia to the northwest coast of North America—tracked by a satellite.

WATER SUPPLY ■ Dolphins don't drink seawater—they obtain all the water they need from the bodies of the fish they eat.

ICE PACK ■ Some American and Chinese alligators can survive the winter by freezing their heads in ice, leaving their nose out to breathe.

TIRE RIDE ■ A cat survived a two-and-a-half-hour truck journey by clinging onto a spare tire. Gil Smith drove 70 mi (113 km) from Gilbert, Arizona, to Kearny, unaware that his cat Bella had climbed onto the tire beneath his truck.

NO BOARD REQUIRED

Deciding that swimming looks like too much hard work, Gentoo penguins in the Falklands took wildlife photographer Andy Rouse by surprise by surfing into shore on top of the waves rather than below them, "I was sitting on the beach laughing at them... it was just awesome." He speculates that they may put on the display in order to escape predators lurking under the breakers, and it might be the best way for them to land under certain conditions in the Falklands where the waves can reach 20 ft (6 m) high. Andy notes that the penguins often swim back out when they reach the beach and surf back in again, suggesting they, like us, do it for the adrenaline rush as well as the practical benefits. Gentoos are the only birds known to catch waves on a regular basis; Andy says Chinstrap penguins tried to copy the Gentoos, but wiped out.

BEAGLE ADVENTURE ■ A dog that went missing in New York mysteriously turned up over five years later in Hinesville, Georgia—more than 850 mi (1,370 km) away. Rocco the beagle slipped under the garden fence of his Queens home in the spring of 2003 and although his owners, the Villacis family, covered the neighborhood with posters, there was no trace of the dog until July 2008, when a Georgia animal shelter was able to return him thanks to an identity microchip under his skin.

CONJOINED SWALLOWS ■ A pair of conjoined barn swallows—a rarity estimated at more than one in a million—was discovered in White County, Arkansas, in July 2008. The birds, which fell out of a nest and died shortly afterward, were fully formed and attached at the hip by skin. At first they appeared to have only three legs, but a fourth leg was found tucked up underneath the connecting skin.

TWO-FACED KITTEN ■ Renee Cook of Amarillo, Texas, found a two-faced kitten among a litter of seven otherwise normal kittens born to her Persian-mixed cat Amber in February 2008. The kitten, which had two mouths, two noses, and four eyes, died the following day.

EXTRA LEGS ■ Hex the kitten was born in Cooper City, Florida, in April 2008 with six legs and two sets of intestines.

CANINE PACEMAKER ■ A dog trained to help authorities search for murder victims and survivors of natural disasters had to be saved herself in May 2008. Search-and-rescue dog Molly, a five-year-old chocolate Labrador retriever from Saginaw, Michigan, was fitted with a pacemaker by veterinarians after suffering a suspected heart attack. Such was Molly's popularity and value to the community that the device was donated by a medical technology company while an anonymous businessman from Kansas paid for most of the surgery fees.

SURVIVED CRUSHER ■ A puppy survived with nothing worse than a bruised paw in 2008—despite being crushed among cardboard in the middle of a garbage truck. A Kentucky recycling company worker found the dog peering out through mangled cardboard after it had been deposited from a truck armed with a ramming device that exerted 35,000 lb (15,875 kg) of pressure.

HELPFUL PARROT ■ When Yosuke the African gray parrot flew out of his cage in Nagareyama, Japan, in 2008 and got lost, he recited his name to his rescuers, just as his owners had taught him to. He told a veterinarian, "I'm Mr. Yosuke Nakamura" and went on to provide his full home address, right down to the street number.

GINGER'S JOURNEY ■ In 2008, a cat survived a 6,500-mi (10,500-km), five-week journey in a shipping container by lapping up condensation. Ginger crept into the container in Taiwan and did not see daylight again until the order of yarn was opened by staff at a textile firm in Nottinghamshire, England.

HELPING PAWS ■ Cavendish, a Leonburger dog, can load the washing machine, pick up items from the floor, and fetch the phone. He is the trusted helper of Dr. Nicola Hendy, a research fellow at England's University of Nottingham, who has cerebral palsy and is blind.

SPORTING GOLDFISH ■ Comet the goldfish can play basketball, soccer and rugby, slalom expertly around a series of poles, play fetch with a hoop, swim through a narrow tube, and even limbo under a miniature bar on the bottom of his tank. The talented goldfish has been trained by Los Angeles computer scientist Dr. Dean Pomerleau, who rewards each correct maneuver with food. He says: "Fish are more intelligent than people give them credit for."

TERRIER TERROR ■ A tiny Yorkshire terrier received the shock of his life in March 2008 after chewing through the wires of a bedside lamp at his home in Lancaster, England. When pup Dylan Thomas was zapped by electricity leaving him stiff and motionless, his owner tried to pull the wire from the animal's mouth, only to be flung across the room by the shock. Emergency chest massage brought the dog back to life and he made a full recovery, despite needing to have part of his frazzled tongue amputated.

ODD COUPLE ■ Although in the wild a goat would be prey for a wolf, the two animals have become sweethearts at a zoo in Nanchong, China. They even share a cage and if the goat decides to wander off for a while, the wolf howls and runs frantically around the cage until she comes back.

DIFFERENT EARS ■ Many species of owl have one ear bigger than the other and one ear higher than the other. This makes it easier for them to judge exactly where a sound is coming from and to pinpoint prey at night.

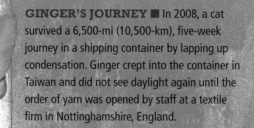

DIFFERENT STINGS ■ A scorpion's first sting is made up of different toxins to its subsequent stings. Whereas the first is usually powerful enough to incapacitate a vertebrate prey or predator, later stings tend to be milder or employed merely to stun smaller invertebrates.

MIRACLE COW ■ A cow in the Indian state of Gujarat releases milk from its udders without any assistance from her owner. The cow—named Radha—produces milk whenever she is fed, delivering 8½ pt (4 l) in the morning and the same amount again in the evening.

I LOVE DOTTIE ■ In March 2008, Dottie, a cat in Sacramento, California, gave birth to a kitten with dark markings on its side that from left to right read "I," then a heart shape, followed by a dot.

TITANIC TONGUE ■ Most elephants weigh less than a blue whale's tongue, which tips the scales at three tons. When fully expanded, a blue whale's mouth can hold 100 tons of food and water, but the dimensions of its throat mean that it is unable to swallow anything wider than a beach ball.

SPITTING VENOM ■ A newly discovered species of spitting cobra from Kenya holds enough venom to kill 15 people.

HUMAN STATUS ■ A woman went to court in 2008 to prove that her chimp deserved human status. Paula Stibbe of Vienna, Austria, argued that Hiasl was like a human child—he loves watching TV and videos, playing games, and can use signs and gestures to indicate what he wants.

SNAKE COLLAR ■ Jelly, a cat owned by Wendy Wallis of Tasmania, Australia, came home one day with a new collar—a highly venomous copperhead snake wrapped around her neck. The reptile was removed by snake wrangler Matthew Stafford and, despite receiving a bite from the poisonous creature, lucky Jelly was soon on the mend after treatment at a local veterinary center.

MYNA MIMIC ■ A myna bird at a shop in Nanjing, China, keeps two noisy parrot neighbors quiet by meowing like a cat. The myna became irritated by the parrots' squawking until it noticed that whenever a cat appeared, they fell silent. Owner Mr. Jiang says: "Whenever the parrots get too noisy, the myna calls their bluff by mimicking the cat, and the parrots hush up right away."

Canine Carts

Two-legged Chihuahuas Venus de Milo, Carmen, and Pablo were featured in Ripley's Believe It or Not! Prepare to be Shocked last year, and we are pleased to report that they are now enjoying life with their new dog carts, provided by the North Shore Animal League of America. The devices help them to move around freely rather than stumbling perilously along on their back legs.

Tremendous Tail

Crystal Socha of Augusta, Kansas, has an equine claim to fame—her 11-year-old American Paint Horse, Summer, has a tail that measures an incredible 12 ft 6 in (3.81 m). The spectacular specimen was shown off during the Equifest of Kansas horse festival in 2008.

SHREW BREW ■ Malaysian tree shrews that drink alcoholic fermented nectar suffer no ill effects from consuming quantities that would inebriate a human. The animals drink daily from the flower buds of a palm. The buds collect yeast, which ferments the nectar to create a potent brew that is 3.8 percent alcohol—as strong as many beers.

HONEY THIEF ■ A bear who repeatedly stole honey from a beekeeper's hives in Macedonia was convicted of theft and criminal damage in March 2008.

MILLIPEDE WALL ■ Villagers in Obereichstaett, Germany, built a specially designed wall in 2007 to keep out the thousands of millipedes that have overrun the town each fall for centuries.

MOUTH-TO-MOUTH ■ The life of a cat trapped in an apartment fire at New Bedford, Massachusetts, in September 2008, was saved when heroic firefighter Al Machado revived the lucky feline using mouth-to-mouth resuscitation.

Prime Mate

Two rare white tiger cubs reared at an animal institute in Myrtle Beach, South Carolina, have an unusual surrogate mother. Anjana, a two-year-old chimpanzee, helped the tiger's keeper to raise Mitra and Shiva since their birth, including feeding them with a bottle. She has also had a hand in caring for leopards, lions and orangutans.

ELEPHANT BAN ■ Twelve-year-old Jack Smithies of the U.K. got 655 people to sign his petition that would allow families to keep elephants as pets in their backyard. However, the British government rejected the 2008 petition on the grounds that elephants were too big and dangerous to be suitable as pets.

BIKER OWL ■ When wildlife-center worker Jenny Smith goes for a ride on her bicycle around the lanes of Staffordshire, England, she has an unusual passenger—a tawny owl called Treacle. He hops on to the handlebars whenever she gets on the bike and stays perfectly still throughout the ride.

PINK POOP ■ Volunteers at a scenic spot in the town of Mansfield in Nottinghamshire, England, painted dog poop bright pink in 2008 in an attempt to shame pet owners into cleaning it up.

BEE ALERT ■ Twelve million swarming bees forced the closure of a California highway in March 2008 after a truck carrying crates of the insects overturned near Sacramento. The bees stung officers, firefighters and tow-truck drivers trying to clear the accident.

MUMMIFIED CAT ■ In December 2008, an Australian man was arrested at an airport in Cairo, Egypt, with a 2,000-year-old mummified cat in his suitcase.

NON-SWIMMER ■ Pfeffer's Flamboyant Cuttlefish, which lives off the coast of Indonesia, walks along the sea floor on its tentacles and fins—because it can't swim.

HEARING ANTLERS ■ Researchers from the University of Guelph, Ontario, Canada, have discovered that a moose's antlers act as giant hearing aids, boosting the animal's hearing by nearly 20 percent. With ears 60 times the size of human ears, moose are renowned for their exceptional hearing, enabling them to hear for distances of up to 2 mi (3.2 km)—but now experiments have shown that antlered bulls can locate moose cows much more accurately than males without antlers or other females.

PRAYERY DOG ■ Conan, a two-year-old Chihuahua, joins in daily prayers at a Buddhist temple in Japan. He sits on his hind legs, raises his paws, and puts them together at the tip of his nose. He has proved so popular with worshipers that attendances have increased by 30 percent since his introduction as temple pet.

The interior of the doghouse, with its themed wallpaper and furnishings, is every bit as stylish as the outside.

Pooch Palaces

A U.S. firm builds luxury houses, complete with air conditioning, custom-made beds, and superbly designed interiors—all for dogs. La Petite Maison designs $50,000 homes for pampered pooches and once built an Alpine chalet for a St. Bernard. In 2008, supermodel Rachel Hunter commissioned a deluxe doghouse that was a scaled-down version of her own Californian home, with terracotta floors and wrought-iron balconies.

KICKBOXING TERRIER ■ A Russian Black Terrier named Ringo Tsar has been learning to kickbox. His owner, former martial arts champion Russ Williams from Holywell, North Wales, has been training the dog to jump up on command and kick at a punch bag with his front legs. He says that while many dogs bite people, Ringo will surely be the first to knock out a human with his paws.

COW ARRESTED ■ A cow was arrested in Cambodia in 2007 for causing traffic accidents that had resulted in the deaths of six people. The cow kept wandering into the road on the outskirts of the capital Phnom Penh, forcing drivers to swerve to avoid it.

SWAN CHAOS ■ Police held up traffic and roads were closed around the town of Langney in East Sussex, England, in June 2008, because a family of swans went on a three-hour walk. Under the Act for Swans introduced back in 1576, no one could touch the birds as they legally belong to the Queen.

PISTOL CRACK ■ Despite being less than 1 inch (2.5 cm) long, the pistol shrimp that swims in the Mediterranean emits a noise measuring 218 decibels—that's louder than a gunshot. The deafening crack is caused by a jet of water that spurts out of the shrimp at 60 mph (100 km/h), creating a bubble that momentarily soars to a temperature of 8,000°F (4,426°C). When the bubble collapses, the surprisingly loud explosion occurs.

SWIMMING CHAMP ■ A water-loving sheepdog named Paris has been made an honorary member of a Chinese swimming club—and even has her own shower cubicle. She swims up to 15 mi (24 km) every day in the Jialing River in Chongqing and has so far swum over 6,500 mi (10,460 km).

JAWS GLUED ■ A dog glued his jaws together after sinking his teeth into a diner menu. Cymbeline, a Scottish Terrier, had been trained to pick up the mail from the doormat of his home in Essex, England, and to hand it to his owner, but the high-gloss paper menu glued his jaws shut for half an hour until a veterinarian managed to free the gum from his teeth.

MUSICAL WALRUS ■ A walrus at a zoo in Turkey has learned to play the saxophone. Sara amazes visitors to the Istanbul Dolphinarium by gripping the instrument between her flippers and blowing out a series of notes.

PET REUNION ■ A woman was reunited with her missing cat in 2008—after nine years. Gilly Delaney from Birmingham, England, thought her beloved pet Dixie had been killed by a car in 1999, so she was amazed when animal welfare officers turned up with the cat after finding it wandering the streets.

SHARK ATTACK ■ A dog in Florida had a lucky escape in 2008 when his owner dived into the water to save him from a 5-ft (1.5-m) shark. Greg LeNoir had taken his Rat Terrier Jake for a swim at the Islamorada marina when the shark surfaced and grabbed the dog in its mouth.

MAN'S BEST FRIEND ■ A German Shepherd dog saved his owner's life in 2008 by hitting the speed-dial button on the phone for 911 to call Emergency and then barking to raise the alarm. Buddy had been trained by his owner, Joe Stalnaker of Scottsdale, Arizona, to act in an emergency.

ENGINE ORDEAL ■ Luna the cat lived to tell the tale after spending a week in the engine of her owner's car in November 2008. She had survived more than 300 mi (480 km) of driving through Austria but had hidden so deep inside the engine that the whole thing had to be dismantled in order to get her out.

TOURISM JOB ■ A chimpanzee in Radkow, Poland, has been given a paid job promoting tourism. Seventeen-year-old Bobby receives $140 a month to walk around with a sign on his back advertising a local beauty spot known as Monkey Rock.

TUNEFUL PARROT ■ Leonard, an African Gray parrot from Bristol, England, has learned to whistle "Dock of the Bay" and the theme tune from *Mission Impossible*. He also does a rendition of "YMCA" by The Village People. His owners describe him as "great fun."

EGG-STREMELY LARGE ■ Children at a school in Gloucester, England, were amazed in January 2009 when their class pet, a hen named Little Lil, laid an egg the size of a tennis ball. The egg, which was three times bigger than normal, measured 4 in (10 cm) from top to bottom and 2¾ in (7 cm) across.

TWO-HEADED FISH ■ Thousands of bass larvae at a fish farm in Noosa River, Queensland, Australia, spawned with two heads. The mutant larvae survived for just 48 hours before they died en masse.

PENGUIN WEDDING ■ An aquarium in Wuhan, China, staged a wedding ceremony for two black-footed penguins in January 2009. The groom, who brought his own tuxedo, was dressed in a tie and his bride wore a red blouse. At the reception, the happy couple dined on their favorite dish—spring fish.

IN A SPIN ■ When spiders are first taken into space, they spin a tangled, messy web—but as they adapt to microgravity, they begin spinning normal, symmetrical webs.

NONSTOP FLIGHT ■ The bar-tailed godwit, a Pacific coastal bird, makes flights of more than 7,000 mi (11,250 km) without stopping to eat.

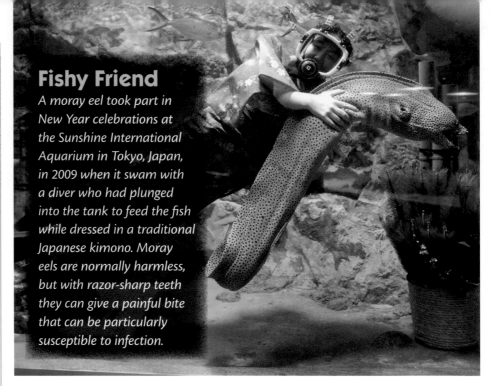

Fishy Friend

A moray eel took part in New Year celebrations at the Sunshine International Aquarium in Tokyo, Japan, in 2009 when it swam with a diver who had plunged into the tank to feed the fish while dressed in a traditional Japanese kimono. Moray eels are normally harmless, but with razor-sharp teeth they can give a painful bite that can be particularly susceptible to infection.

DOGGY WIGS ■ A Santa Barbara, California, firm called Total Diva Pets sells a range of $30 hairpieces for dogs. Sisters Jenny and Crissy Slaughter sell the doggy wigs in eight different designs—including Afro and green spiky punk—and in five sizes from Chihuahua to Great Dane.

OCTOPUS VANDAL ■ Otto, an octopus at the Star Aquarium in Coburg, Germany, caused electrical short circuits by crawling to the rim of his tank and squirting a jet of water at a light fixture.

BEASTLY BEETLE ■ A species of Peruvian dung beetle has turned from scavenger to carnivore. Whereas it once ate only animal feces, the ferocious scarab has been observed decapitating and eating live millipedes ten times its size.

SINGING FISH ■ Researchers at Indiana University have discovered that the art of singing originated in lungfish. They say that the pattern of beak and throat movements in birds, as well as mouth, tongue and lower-jaw motions in humans, all started to evolve when lungfish began gulping and swallowing air.

AQUAPHOBIC PENGUIN ■ A penguin at the Blackbrook Zoological Park in Staffordshire, England, has become a celebrity because he is afraid of water. While his 23 penguin pals swim around happily, Kentucky stands on a rock and refuses to take the plunge. Keepers say the Humboldt penguin was born smaller than his siblings and has lost a lot of feathers since birth, which might make the water a bit cold for him.

KEEN VISION ■ Jumping spiders of the genus Portia have incredible vision for their small size. Their tiny primary eyes have better visual acuity than lizards, pigeons or cats.

NEVER TOO OLD ■ A reptile in New Zealand has become a father at the age of 111. Henry, a tuatara living at the Southland Museum and Art Gallery, was aggressive toward female lizards until having a cancerous growth removed from his genitals in 2002. Since then, he has mellowed and after mating with a female named Mildred, he became the proud father of 11 baby tuataras.

Two-faced Cow

A young calf born with two faces due to a genetic abnormality attracted attention from locals in Lintao county, China, in 2007 because it had four eyes and two mouths.

FUN ANIMALS

Ripley's **Believe It or Not!®**

When elephants carried cameras hidden in logs into the jungle, some creatures were intrigued to see their reflection in the glass, while others, such as the rare Bengal tigers (below), barely noticed them at all.

ELEPHANT CAM

Elephants at Pench National Park in Madhya Pradesh, India, were specially trained as over-sized cameramen for a TV documentary. The elephants were hired to carry the cameras, which had been disguised as logs and rocks, with their tusks and trunks, and walked deep into the jungle where they captured some unparalleled images of elusive Bengal tigers. Wild tigers are used to sharing their habitat with elephants, so they were oblivious to the filming, viewing the cameras with mild curiosity rather than suspicion.

Bulging Belly

A bulge in a python's belly was all that could be seen of 8-week-old tabby cat Kohl after he was swallowed whole in the garden of the McLaren family in Darwin in Australia's Northern Territory in 2008. X-ray photographs taken after the 6-ft-long (1.8-m) snake was removed clearly show the kitten stretched out inside its stomach. The unfortunate pet was swallowed by the hungry snake despite having a head three times as large as that of the python.

FUN ANIMALS

www.ripleys.com

Ripley's — Believe It or Not!®

DEVOTED MOM ■ When her six little ducklings were swept down a drain cover in Newcastle upon Tyne, England, in 2008, a mother mallard duck followed their panicked cheeps for more than a mile (1.6 km)—across roads, traffic circles, train lines, two school fields, and the grounds of a hospital.

DOG SPARED ■ Ordered to be put down after attacking a child, Ozzy the German shepherd had his sentence commuted to life imprisonment in 2007—and landed a job patrolling the perimeter of a correctional facility near Media, Pennsylvania.

SNAKE SCARE ■ Hearing her baby cry, Cari Abatemarco peered into the crib at the family home in Brentwood, New York—and found a 12-in (30-cm), non-venomous kingsnake wrapped around her seven-month-old daughter's leg.

RUBBLE RESCUE ■ A dog was found alive in April 2008 having spent eight days trapped beneath 15 ft (4.5 m) of rubble after a two-story building exploded in Breckenridge, Colorado. Springer Spaniel Lulu survived the ordeal by drinking melting snow and eating food she found in the debris.

SURPRISE PACKAGE ■ A cat was accidentally posted 450 mi (725 km) in 2008 after it crawled unnoticed into a parcel and fell asleep. Gitti Rauch from Rottach-Egern in southern Germany said her cat climbed into a box filled with presents for relatives in Dorsten, but she didn't spot him as she sealed the package and sent it off. Janosch emerged unharmed two days later.

BATHTUB ORDEAL ■ A four-year-old cat from Stadthagen, Germany, survived despite being walled in beneath a bathtub for seven weeks. She lost 9 lb (4 kg) during her ordeal.

HEROIC PARROT ■ A parrot saved his owners from a house fire in July 2008 by squawking loudly enough to raise the alarm. Bob, a three-year-old African gray, alerted the Hall family that fire was spreading through their house in Hampshire, England. Thanks to Bob, the Halls managed to flee the blaze in time, grabbing their savior's cage on the way out. Sam Hall said: "I used to find Bob very annoying with his growling and squawking, but not now. He's a legend. He saved our lives."

BEAR SAVED ■ A 364-lb (165-kg) black bear that had been shot with a tranquilizer dart was saved from drowning in 2008 by a wildlife officer who dived into the sea to rescue it. Seeing the drowsy bear run into the water, Adam Warwick of the Florida Fish and Wildlife Commission stripped to his underwear, swam out to sea and put his arm around the animal's neck to keep its head above water.

SIZZLING SNAKE ■ A snake was treated for third-degree burns in Australia in 2008 after hitching a ride under the hood of a car. The 8-ft (2.4-m) python had wrapped itself around the car radiator for warmth, but was then taken by surprise when the vehicle embarked on a long journey from northern New South Wales. The overheated car broke down and when the owner looked under the hood, he was shocked to find a broken fan belt—and a very hot and very cranky snake.

Hungry Heron

Known to eat small mammals and frogs, this hungry Gray Heron horrified onlookers in Vianen, Holland, when it made a grab for a baby rabbit on the banks of a river. The squealing creature was carried to the water, quickly drowned, and much to the disbelief of onlookers, swallowed whole!

LAUNDRY SHOCK ■ Removing clothes from the washing machine at her home in Gorham, Maine, in July 2008, Mara Ranger was horrified to find an 8-ft (2.4-m) reticulated python among her laundry. The snake is believed to have entered the machine through water pipes. It was removed by an officer from the local animal control department before being taken to New York's Wild Animal Kingdom.

RAGING BULL ■ A bull that was swept into a raging river during floods in Australia in January 2008 survived a 56-mi (90-km) trip downstream with tree trunks, logs and fences before being rescued. Two-year-old Barney was found in an exhausted state at the mouth of the Tweed River near the ocean in New South Wales.

DEER SURGEON ■ John Polson of Saskatoon, Canada, performed a roadside cesarean section on a white-tailed deer in 2008. Spotting a deer alive but badly injured beside a vehicle, he decided to end the animal's suffering and then remembered that it was the season for female deer to be giving birth. So he cut open her womb, discovered two live fawns and took them home to be hand-reared before being released back into the wild.

BUNNY ALARM ■ A pet rabbit—named Rabbit—saved a couple from a fire in Melbourne, Australia, in 2008 by scratching furiously on their bedroom door to wake them as they slept while smoke poured through the house. The six-month-old floppy-eared rabbit was allowed to roam the house unless its owners, Gerry Keogh and his partner Michelle Finn, had guests. Firefighters went back into the burning building to rescue the heroic pet, because the smoke had prevented its owners from finding him.

PIG BOOTS ■ A piglet in North Yorkshire, England, was fitted with little rain boots in 2008 so that she could conquer her fear of mud. When the piglet appeared reluctant to get her trotters dirty, Debbie and Andrew Keeble solved the problem by giving her four miniature rain boots that had served as novelty pen and pencil holders in their office.

SNAIL COMPANION ■ A Chinese man is so devoted to his pet snail that he takes it for walks. Yang Jinsen from Dongwan, found the snail by the roadside on his way home from school in 1997 and has looked after it ever since, building it a nice home, playing with it, taking it for walks in the fields and, in 2007, introducing it to his new wife. The snail has responded to the loving care by living for more than twice its normal life span.

DONKEY JAILED ■ A donkey spent three days in a Mexican jail in May 2008 after it bit and kicked two men in Chiapas State. It was released from the prison, which normally houses drunks, when its owner paid a fine and the injured men's medical bills.

DONKEY RETIRES ■ Russia's prestigious Mariinsky ballet bade farewell to one of its longest-serving artistes in 2008—a 21-year-old donkey named Monika. Pensioned off after 19 years of carrying the overweight Sancho Panza around the stage in productions of *Don Quixote*, at her retirement party she danced a waltz with one of the company's ballerinas and was presented with a carrot cake.

HAMSTER HUNT ■ Roborovski's hamster, a native of northern China, forages so keenly for food that in a single night it covers over 100 mi (160 km)—a distance equivalent to almost four human marathons.

ELECTRIC ANTS ■ Many ant species nest near electrical equipment owing to an affinity for magnetic fields created by electricity.

SAVINGS EATEN ■ An Indian trader lost his life savings after the paper bills were eaten by termites infesting the bank's safe deposit boxes. Dwarika Prasad had deposited more than $16,000 with the Central Bank of India in 2005, but when he opened the box in January 2008, there was little more than termite dust.

HEAT DETECTORS ■ The heat-sensitive pit located on each side of a rattlesnake's head enables it to detect items of prey that are as little as one-tenth of a degree warmer than the environment around them.

PIGEON SERVICE ■ A pigeon called Spitfire—capable of flying at speeds of up to 60 mph (95 km/h)—is used by Rocky Mountain Adventures in Colorado to carry memory cards containing pictures of white-water rafters back to base so that the day-trippers' photographs can be developed in time for them to take home.

BLOOD DONOR ■ The American Red Cross honored one of its most unusual blood donors in February 2008—a 200-lb (90-kg), two-year-old English Mastiff named Lurch. Owned by Joni Melvin-Thiede from Howell, Michigan, Lurch has donated blood more than 20 times, helping to save the lives of dozens of dogs.

TIGHTROPE WALKER ■ In Chongqing City, China, in 2008, a two-year-old Tibetan Mastiff called Hu Hu demonstrated his skill as a high-wire artist. The dog climbed to the top of a platform 13 ft (4 m) high and, balancing his paws on two thin steel wires, walked 33 ft (10 m) to the other side.

UPSIDE DOWN ■ Africa's mochokid catfish can swim upside down to enable it to feed on the underside of rocks and branches that have fallen underwater.

HOSE ESCAPE ■ A spider monkey briefly escaped from Washington Park Zoo in Michigan City, Indiana, in 2008 by climbing up a garden hose left there while workers were cleaning a moat. He was recaptured at a nearby boat dealership, perched on top of a speedboat.

RELIGIOUS BUZZ ■ Beekeeper Slobodan Jeftic from Stari Kostolac, Serbia, builds beehives in the shape of tiny monasteries and churches so that, besides giving his bees somewhere beautiful to live and make honey, he can look after their souls.

SOLDIER BEAR ■ During World War II, a brown bear named Voytek captured a spy in Iraq and helped transport ammunition in Italy for the Polish Army. The 250-lb (115-kg) bear, who stood more than 6 ft (1.8 m) tall, was such a valued member of the armed forces that he was given his own name, rank, and number. Like most other soldiers of that era, he enjoyed a beer and a cigarette when off duty.

DOGGIE SCHNAUZER, M.D. ■ A dog has predicted the deaths of 40 people at a Canton, Ohio, nursing home over a three-year period. Staff noticed that Skamp the schnauzer seems to know when people are about to die and will spend hours, even a couple of days, with a dying resident.

CAT LOVER ■ A dog risked his life to save a litter of newborn kittens from a house fire in Melbourne, Australia, in October 2008. Leo, a Terrier cross, refused to leave the burning building without the four kittens—and after his bravery he had to be revived with oxygen and heart massage. Happily, the kittens also survived.

LUCKY KOALA ■ A koala bear survived being hit by a car at 60 mph (97 km/h) and dragged with his head jammed through the grill for 8 mi (12 km). The eight-year-old bear was struck north of Brisbane in Queensland, Australia, in July 2008 and was freed only after the car was flagged down by another motorist.

Gerbil Power

Super Pet has created the "Critter Cruiser" for pet gerbils who are bored with going round and round the wheels in their cages. The cruiser is a fully gerbil-powered car that enables our furry friends to race around a specially designed track, going as fast or slow as they like.

Blowing Bubbles

Dolphins are known as the playful animals of the sea, but visitors to an Orlando sea-life center were amazed to see them making bubble rings with an expert touch before following them through the water. The dolphins create the bubbles by churning the water in swift movements and blowing through their blowhole, swimming through the rings and nosing them into different shapes. They will even make more than one ring and join them together, apparently all just for fun.

Index

Page numbers in *italics* refer to illustrations

ACKNOWLEDGMENTS

COVER (l) Richard Austin/Rex Features, (t/r) California Academy of Sciences, (b/r) Chris Van Wyk; BACK COVER www.firebox.com; 4 Chris Van Wyk; 6 (t/l) Paul A. Zahl/National Geographic/Getty Images, (t/r) © NHPA/Photoshot, (b/l, b/r) Chris Van Wyk; 7 Steven Haddock/ MBARI; 8 (t) Newspix/Rex Features, (b) WENN/Newscom; 9 (t, r) Rick Scibelli/Getty Images, (sp) © alle - Fotolia.com; 10 Feature China/ Barcroft Media; 11 *MaxPPP*/Photoshot; 12–13 Zoom/Barcroft Media; 14 (t) Newspix/Rex Features, (b) David Scholnick & Lou Burnett; 15 (t) Barcroft Pacific, (b) Mark Clifford/Barcroft Media; 16 Feature China/ Barcroft Media; 17 (t) California Academy of Sciences, (b) Richard Austin/Rex Features; 18 Otago Museum Dunedin New Zealand; 19 (t) SWNS.com, (b) Chris Van Wyk; 20–21 Kiyoshi Ota/Getty Images; 22 Newspix/Rex Features; 23 (t, c) Andy Rouse/Rex Features, (b) Andy Rouse/NHPA/Photoshot; 24–25 (b) Stephen Douglass/Rex Features; 25 (r) Gary Roberts/Rex Features; 26 (t) Mike Hutmacher/AP/PA Photos, (b) Barry Bland/Barcroft Media; 27 La Petite Maison/Solent News/ Rex Features; 28 (t) Reuters/Yuriko Nakao, (b) Tian Xi/ChinaFotoPress/Photocome/PA Photos; 29 John Downer Productions; 30 Newspix/ Rex Features; 31 © UPPA/Photoshot; 32 www.firebox.com; 33 Barry Bland/Barcroft Media

Key: t = top, b = bottom, c = center, l = left, r = right, sp = single page, dp = double page

All other photos are from Ripley Entertainment Inc.
Every attempt has been made to acknowledge correctly and contact copyright holders and we apologize in advance
for any unintentional errors or omissions, which will be corrected in future editions.